D0405507

Dear Parents,

Is your child a new reader? If yes, one good way to help your child build confidence and word recognition skills is by introducing word families.

The die-cuts at the bottoms of the pages draw attention to three different word families (letters show through each die-cut shape).

Once your child can read "**op**", then he or she can focus on the beginning letters and sounds:

stop, pop, cop, top, pop

After the single words are learned, the pictures help your child read the words in phrases:

pop on top   **stop on top**
cop on top of pop   **top cop**

It's much easier to learn a group of words than to memorize them by sight one word at a time. A sight vocabulary is limited by the number of words that can be held in memory.

Recognizing words by families hugely increases the number of words that your child can know. It gives your child a way to sound out new words (reading specialists call these "word attack" skills), thereby increasing the likelihood he or she will feel successful.

Help your child with the 25 new words in this book by giving him or her multiple chances to read it until all the words are mastered.

Most important, have fun together!

Harriet Ziefert, M.A.
Language Arts/Reading Specialist

Ziefert, Harriet.
Stop pop /
2007.

cu   07/03/18

Pop

by **Harriet Ziefert**

Illustrated by **Yukiko Kido**

flip-a

WORD

Word Families

The world is full of print. Written words are everywhere. It's impossible to learn printed words by memorizing them word, by word, by word. To make learning easier, words can be grouped into families.

The words in a word family have two or more letters that are the same. We read "op" words and "un" words, "it" words and "an" words. If you know "op," then it's easier to learn top, pop, and stop.

This book has words from three different word families. All the words in a family rhyme—which means you can add other words to the group by changing the first letter.

It's okay if some of the words you think of are not real words. If you make "nop" or "dop" or "zop," it's not wrong— as long as you know the difference between a real word and a nonsense word.

Flip each page and presto-change-o— a new word appears!

The

Family

c
n
k
m
g
p
h
r
d
s
w

top

C

pop

cop on top of pop

stop on top

top cop

The

un

Family

f
l
w
m
g
n
b
r
d
w
t

bun

r

fun

run bun, run

fun to run

fun in the sun

The

an

Family

f
l
w
m
g
n
b
r
d
w
t

man

C

f

tan

tan man

tan fan

man with fan

fan on can

The op Family

cop	pop
crop	shop
drop	stop
lop	top

The un Family

bun	run
fun	stun
pun	sun

The an Family

ban	man
bran	pan
can	plan
fan	tan

Find the words in each family.

stop

man

sun

run

bun

tan

cop

drop

shop

can

stun

top

man

plan

run

can

drop

stun

pop

bran

lop

crop

drop

stop

cop

tan

fun

pan

lop

man

bun

ban

shop

fun

man

plan

cop

sun

tan

bran

fan

pun

top

Word Family Activities

- Choose two words from the word family and make your own "flip-a-word" illustrations. Remember to make a cut-out at the bottom of the page where the word family shows through.

- Words in a word family rhyme. Learn a song or a poem that rhymes and share it. Or read a book that rhymes and guess which words rhyme.

- Write or tell or draw a story using two or three of the characters in this book. What happens next?